Did you know?

A little book to remind you of just how big of a deal you are!

by Sarah Barney

Balboa Press books may be ordered through booksellers or by contacting:

Balboa Press
A Division of Hay House
1663 Liberty Drive
Bloomington, IN 47403
www.balboapress.com
844-682-1282

ISBN: 979-8-7652-3586-7 (sc)
ISBN: 979-8-7652-3585-0 (e)

Print information available on the last page.

Balboa Press rev. date: 10/28/2022

BALBOA.PRESS
A DIVISION OF HAY HOUSE

I am a child of God.

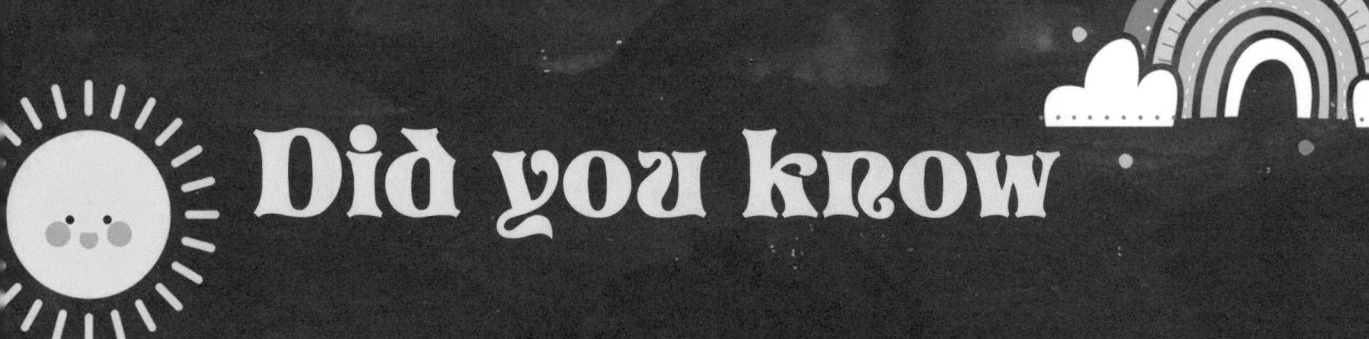

Did you know

- that you are a daughter or son of God?
- that He created you exactly the way you are on purpose?

God doesn't make mistakes.

If He wanted you to be taller or shorter, to have blue eyes or brown eyes, or to have light skin or dark skin, then He would have made you that way!

Who you are, and how you are, is perfect!

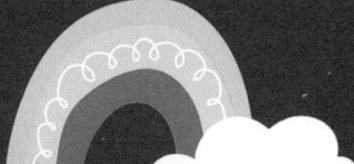

I am equipped with everything I need.

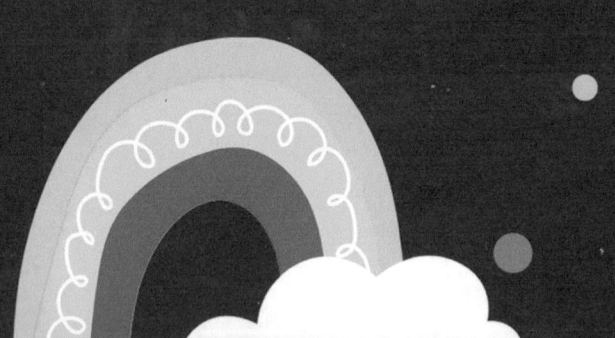

Did you know

- that everything you need to have, in order to be who you really want to be, is already inside you?

You don't need to look to other people or things to become who you already are.

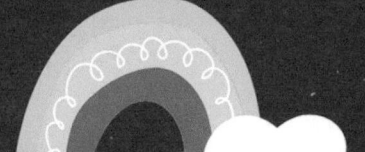

I am capable of doing big things because I am His child.

Did you know

- that since you are a child of God, you have godlike qualities in you?

I am a masterpiece.
I am an original.
I am priceless.

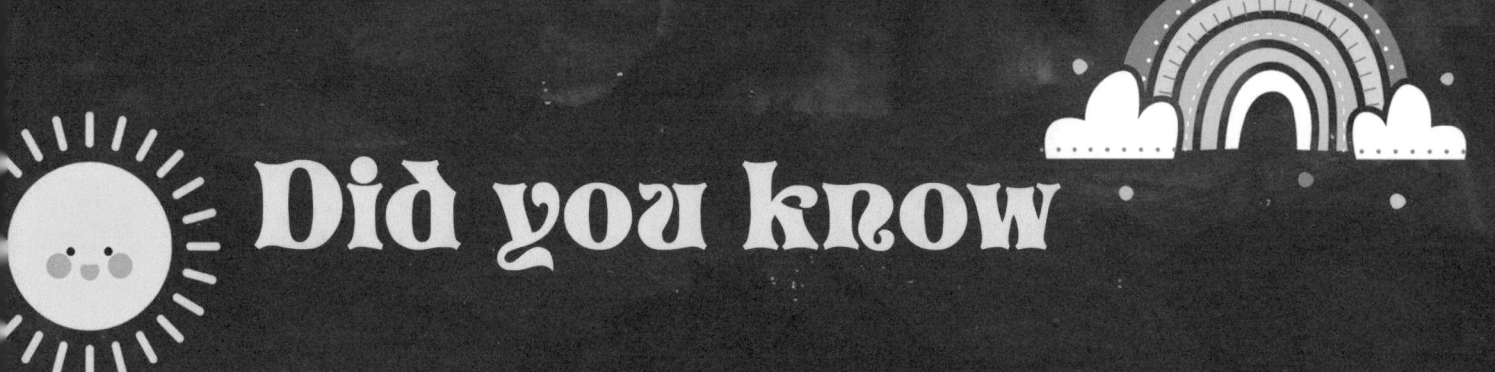

Did you know

- people pay a lot of money for original pieces of art but not much for copies of the original?

Did you know that there is *no one* else like you in the whole world?

You are unique and one of a kind.

I believe in myself.
I am unstoppable.

Did you know the following?

- If you tell yourself, *"I can!"* then *you can!*

- If you tell yourself, *"I can't!"* then *you can't!*

Which one do you want to believe?

Believe *you can,* and you will be unstoppable!

I am stronger than the challenges that come my way.
I can do hard things.

Did you know

- you were built to do and overcome hard things?

If you think of all the hard moments, or days, you have had in your life so far, you have overcome them all!

You got this!

You can easily cut these next affirmations out and put them on both your wall and mirror to help you have an amazing day or to help you get through a not-so-good day.

I can do hard things.

I am doing a great job.

I am making myself proud.

I am good enough.

I am beautiful.

I am kind.

I am honest.

I am confident.

I am a good person.

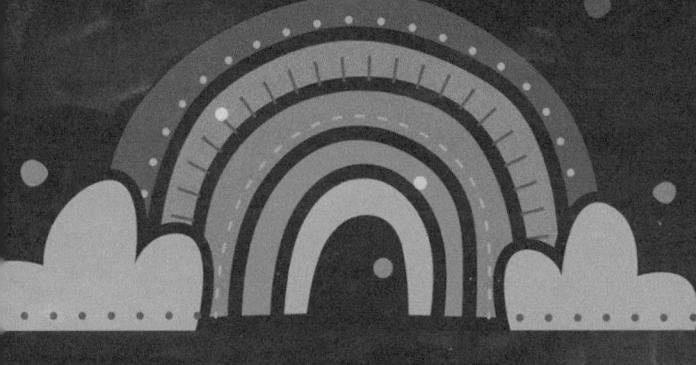

I am a peacemaker.

I am a wave maker.

I am compassionate.

I am powerful.

I am a good listener.

I am strong.

I am true to who I am.

I am calm and relaxed.

I am good under pressure.

I am in control of myself.

I am courageous.

I am smart.

I am funny.

I am creative.

I am brave.

I am a good helper.

I am love.

I am a hard worker.

I am light.

Printed in the United States
by Baker & Taylor Publisher Services